Clean Water, Red Wine, Broken Bread

*A Short Invitation
to the Christian Faith*

Douglas Wilson, *Clean Water, Red Wine, Broken Bread*
©2000 by Christ Church, P.O. Box 8729, Moscow, ID 83843.

ISBN: 1-885767-68-4

20 21 22   4 3 2

Hunger

To the extent we think we have any problems at all, we all like to think of ourselves as poor, misunderstood souls. We *mean* well, and all the trouble we bring to others is the result of mysterious and inscrutable causes. Springsteen had a "wife and kids in Baltimore, Jack," and so he went out for a ride and he never went back. All this in an attempt to satisfy a hungry heart.

In a real way, we *do* have hungry hearts. But this is because we believe that bread can be made out of sawdust—we think that fidelity can be manufactured out of treachery, and that our self-absorbtion can, by some strange alchemy, be turned into altruism. We are spiritually hungry, but the reason for this is that we continue to refuse to eat the food God has prepared for us. It is not that a famine has been imposed upon us from the outside, but rather we are hungry because of our distaste for wholesome food.

This booklet is written with the assumption that the reader knows something of the radical nature of the problem with people. He may not know why this is the case, or the extent of the disaster, and he may not believe the situation is any better within the Christian faith, but at least he knows the problem is there. There will consequently be no attempt at flattery.

The Scriptures describe the human race as radically sinful—or, to use a non-theological term, we are pigs. It might be more rhetorically effective to save this for later, but if the image of God is to be restored in us, we need to face the problem honestly. And if we do, the point must come when we recognize how far we have fallen and how brutish we have become. In desperate circumstances, dishonesty is always deadly. Nothing can be gained by nursing sentimental views of human nature. We have a problem, and anyone who denies the problem cannot have the solution.

But this case can be made effectively enough to make us wonder if the Christian faith can really present any alternative. If men and women are *that* depraved, then it would stand to reason that they would corrupt everything they touch, including every churchy thing they touch. And the data appears to support this—Christian behavior on television certainly does not inspire confidence in the dignity of our species. Instead we find a bizarre stew of head slapping, keeling over, gold furniture, mile-high hair, words of knowledge, sappy songs, biblical ignorance, and all done in the name of Jesus Christ, praise God. If the human race is as bad as it appears to be, how *could* it be possible for the Christian faith to avoid being part of the general bedlam? So this brings us to begin with the problem of the hypocrite.

Clearing Away Some Debris

There is nothing worse than a bad time at church. And from the reports, it appears that many non-Christians have had some really bad experiences with the church. As a result, when these non-believers glance in the direction of Christ, on many occasions the view is obstructed by the "problem of the hypocrite."

For such non-believers, the problem of hypocrisy in

the church appears to be an insurmountable one. Plainly, it seems, hypocrisy reveals Christianity for what it really is—a broad collection of sanctimonious liars tied together in fellowship with a common set of superficial platitudes, which are promptly forgotten when the car door slams shut in the church parking lot.

Here is the problem. We have all seen instances of true hypocrisy. What are we to make of it when pastors run off with other people's wives, when scandal surrounds the handling of finances by various ministries, or even when someone with a "Jesus is Lord" bumper sticker gives another motorist twenty-percent of a wave? All of these people call themselves Christians, and why should any self-respecting non-Christian want to be like them?

The short answer is that he should continue in his desire not to be like them. When we turn to the Bible, we find that hypocrites are treated with an imperfect tenderness.

> Woe unto you, scribes and Pharisees, hypocrites! for ye are like unto whited sepulchres, which indeed appear beautiful outward, but are within full of dead men's bones, and of all uncleanness. Even so ye also outwardly appear righteous unto men, but within ye are full of hypocrisy and iniquity (Matt. 23:27-28).

If we examine this passage (and every other passage on hypocrisy in the Bible), we find that hypocrisy is universally and roundly condemned. In no place does God praise the hypocrite. No where does God encourage the fakes to keep it up through promises of great reward at the day of judgment. When Christ said His followers were the light of the world, this did not mean that they were to shine the world on.

Bluntly stated, this means that God and the hypocrite

are on *opposite sides*. God is opposed to the hypocrite, and the hypocrite is opposed to God. Now what does this mean? What is any non-believer who wields the "problem of hypocrisy" actually doing? He is refusing to serve God, continuing to oppose God, because the hypocrite also is opposing God. He continues to stay away from God because he dislikes how the hypocrites stay away from God. He hates the hypocrite, and so he stands shoulder to shoulder with him. This makes no sense whatever. This is like a citizen of one country refusing to become a citizen of another because it is infested with spies from the first country. Should we really applaud when someone refuses to join the other side because of obnoxious things people on his own side are doing? Using the short form, if there is a hypocrite between an individual and God, then obviously that individual is too far away from God.

The Bible goes on to teach that the hypocrite and the outside objector play off each other. Like two drowning swimmers clutching at each other, they both sink under the judgment of God. In the book of Romans, Paul first addresses, and condemns, the hypocrite.

> Thou therefore which teachest another, teachest thou not thyself? thou that preachest a man should not steal, dost thou steal? Thou that sayest a man should not commit adultery, dost thou commit adultery? thou that abhorrest idols, dost thou commit sacrilege? Thou that makest thy boast of the law, through breaking the law dishonourest thou God? (Rom. 2:21-23)

He then refers to those outside this arena of hypocrisy, those mocking the name of God because of real hypocrisy. "For the name of God is blasphemed among the Gentiles through you, as it is written" (Rom. 2:24). Obviously, it is a sin to blaspheme the name of God for any reason. But it is understood in Scripture that sinful men will seize upon the excuse of hypocrisy in others in order to continue their own rebellion against God. This blasphemy will be judged right alongside the hypocrisy. If God were to judge our sins alphabetically, then hypocrisy would be judged in between *greed* and *idolatry*.

Hypocrisy does present a problem for the church, but it is the same kind of pastoral problem as those which result from other sins among the members of the church. It is a disciplinary problem and not a problem for Christian apologetics at all.

What must be done with real hypocrites? We must at once limit our answer to real hypocrites who have been exposed in that hypocrisy. The Lord Jesus has given His people no warrant to attempt to peer into the hearts of others. The pretence of being able to do so is itself a species of hypocrisy. So then, what is to be done with someone who has made an open profession of faith in Jesus Christ and has an equally open problem with sin? The biblical answer to this is formal church discipline. Such a person must be put outside of the church where he belongs. And under church discipline, he must be sent out to join his brothers in rebellion—those who refuse to come to Christ because of "all the hypocrites in church."

This brings us down to the point. The non-believer who is considering the Christian faith must avoid taking his view of it from scoundrels and charlatans. This means two things. First, he should consider the Christian gospel only when it is presented in a way faithful to the teaching of the Scriptures. And secondly, he should take care to study the question in some depth. The doctrine must be faithful all the way down. Every teaching that contradicts Scripture must be rejected, as well as teaching that merely rests lightly upon the surface of the Scriptures.

A Standing Invitation

The Christian faith proclaims a standing invitation to a grand and glorious banquet. But those who wish to attend this feast must first be washed. This washing is declared by the clean water of baptism. After we are washed, we may sit down at the Lord's Supper, consisting of red wine and broken bread. All these things are explained in the Christian message of salvation, which the bread and the wine in turn declare and embody in another way. These two sacraments are an embodiment of the gospel and provide us with our title—clean water, red wine, and broken bread.

The purpose here is to provide a preliminary explanation of this salvation for thoughtful inquirers. An invitation to this banquet is too gracious to be dismissed out of hand, and it is too profound to accept glibly. The Christian faith is a serious and demanding religion founded on the gladness and delight of God. Given this, it should be obvious that a proper understanding of this faith cannot really be acquired through reading the occasional bumper sticker, billboard, or tract. Because the Christian faith is in fact a *faith*, an all-encompassing worldview, it cannot be reduced to cute little slogans. At the same time, an intelligent initial interest in Christianity does not require graduate level study of all the doctrines, practices, and history of the Christian faith.

Consequently, it is my hope that this booklet may serve as a *starting* point for those who, for various reasons, have decided to begin taking the invitation to Christian faith seriously. In doing this, I have sought to avoid two common practices: assuming that non-Christians are familiar with Christian jargon and using terms like "born again," without explaining what that is, and "dumbing down" the faith, emptying it of all specific content. My assumption is that the reader is an intelligent non-believer who wants neither to be patronized nor snowed.

The Lord Jesus told His followers to preach the good news of His kingdom to every creature. This assigned mission is near the center of the Church's very reason for existence in this world. The message, this good news, is called the gospel, and the purpose of this booklet is to explain that gospel and to invite men to respond to it. So what is this "gospel," and why is it considered good news?

The condition and situation of readers will of course vary. Some of you readers may not be Christians, but believe you are. Some of you may know you are not Christians, but have no real idea of what you really believe about God. Some may be non-Christians who hold to another set of definite convictions—Islam or Judaism for example. A few may have been transformed by the gospel, but don't know what has happened to you. Others of you are in the very common situation of having been baptized at some point in their lives, and yet your beliefs are not at all Christian. Your baptism says one thing, but you have come to say another. But in all such cases, the need to grasp the rudiments of the Christian faith remains the same. This means that we should now give ourselves in earnest to the task of understanding.

Given the nature of the case, the facts of the gospel will first be set out in a straightforward and explanatory way. But once the terms of God's gracious offer are well understood, a time always comes when men must respond to that offer, one way or the other. And at that point, the tone of this booklet will necessarily change. Knowing what it is to fear God, Paul said, we seek to persuade men. And so we do.

A Deep Covenant

Central to an understanding of the gospel is a comprehension of God's *covenant* with Adam, who was the head of the human race. Having said this, we must define the word *covenant*. A covenant is a solemn, binding agreement, sovereignly administered, with attendant blessings and curses. Human history began with a covenant; all the elements of a covenant were present in the Garden of Eden. Adam was solemnly forbidden by His Creator to eat from a tree. The prohibition was given in the midst of blessing, and he was warned of the possible curse. He was told that the day he ate of the tree in the middle of the garden, he would surely *die*.

> And the LORD God commanded the man, saying, "Of every tree of the garden you may freely eat; but of the tree of the knowledge of good and evil you shall not eat, for in the day that you eat of it *you shall surely die.*" (Gen. 2:16-17)

In the account that follows, we see that Adam disobeyed God. But more was involved in this than simple disobedience. Adam also became, at that point, a covenant breaker. This point is made later in the Bible, when the prophet Hosea is rebuking the disobedient men of his own day. He compares them to Adam, the first man—"But like [Adam] *they transgressed the covenant*; there they dealt treacherously with Me" (Hos. 6:7).

This brings us to an important point: *sin breaks something.* Too many people think of sin simply as something which is somehow "wrong" and leave it at that. But God had established a relationship with Adam that was a covenant relationship, and in defying His command, Adam was assaulting that relationship. When the fellowship between God and man was severed, we say that the covenant between them was broken.

So Adam broke his covenant with God. But why have I called it a "deep covenant"? God's covenant with Adam was a deep covenant because we, as Adam's offspring, are implicated in it, though separated from him by many generations. Our union with Adam is an organic one, and this means that when Adam broke the covenant, we also broke the covenant. When Adam attacked his relationship with God, we attacked our relationship with God. What he did, *we* did.

God had told Adam that if he disobeyed and ate the fruit of the forbidden tree, he would surely die. But was this warning limited simply to Adam as an individual? Adam was a single man, true enough, but we must also note that at his creation, Adam also *was* the entire human race. When Eve was created, Adam was the head of his family. But he was also the head of the whole human race. In a very real sense, he was humanity.

So when God threatened death for disobedience, to whom was He speaking? Surely the question can be answered by looking at how God fulfilled His Word. Was Adam the only one to die? If not, then we can see how God was speaking to us as well—to every human being who dies. When God spoke this warning, Eve had not yet been created, and you and I were not yet born. But we were all there *by covenant,* and so we were all bound to refrain from eating the fruit. This is why we die—we die because God always keeps His word. If we really were not there in any sense, then the sentence of death would not rest upon us. But it does rest upon us. Every reader of these words will one day die. The hands that hold these pages will one day be motionless bones. Death can therefore be understood as the identifying mark of all covenant breakers. If we die, then we broke covenant with God through our father Adam.

In the New Testament, Paul makes this same point about how death came into this unhappy world — "Therefore, just as through one man sin entered the world, and death through sin, and thus death spread to all men, because all sinned. . ." (Rom. 5:12). All men sin because one man sinned, and all men die because one man sinned. This is not unjust, because Adam was the representative head of everyone who is descended from him. In Adam everyone sinned, and in Adam everyone died. The family resemblance continues down to the present day; just like Adam we all sin, and just like Adam we all die.

So we see that man has a terminal problem. But before a proposed solution will make any sense at all, we must correctly assess the *nature* of our problem. If you have read this far, you are at least interested in the subject of salvation. This is an important subject for an individual to consider because individuals are saved "by ones." But this obvious fact has led some into a serious confusion. Individuals are to be saved, but not in an individualistic way. As a race, we were plunged into sin corporately and covenantally, and we can only be brought out of our sin in the same way. Put another way, an Adam got us into this mess, and so another Adam has to get us out.

This is why the apostle Paul talks about our salvation *by comparing Adams* — "For as in Adam all die, even so in Christ all shall be made alive" (1 Cor. 15:22). Those who are made alive by Christ are made alive in *the same kind of way* that they were made dead in Adam. Refusal to see what God has taught us about how we got *into* our sin is what blinds us to the only provision which He has made for us to get *out*. The way *in* is similar to the way *out*. We did not sin our way into death individually, and we will not believe our way out of death individually. We were lost in Adam; we are saved in another Adam, the Lord Jesus.

When Adam became a covenant breaker, the whole race, represented in him, became a covenant-breaking race. Because we had violated the covenant which defined our necessary *lifelink* with God, this meant that human nature, now separated from God, was violently thrown into a kind of spiritual death. Man was created for fellowship with God, but with this sort of enmity between us and God, our *nature* was altered. What used to be straight was now bent, and what used to be free was now enslaved. Most importantly, what used to be spiritually alive was now dead.

But it is important for us to understand what this death means. It does *not* mean that we were turned into spiritual blocks of wood. It means that we are separated from God, and that we have no way of getting across this spiritual chasm ourselves. Just as physical death is the *separation* of the soul from the body, so spiritual death should be understood as the separation of man from God.

In this condition, enough of "the image of God" remains with us that we are embarrassed by our sins—we are ashamed, sometimes, by what we *do*. But because there is very little understanding of the Bible's teaching on this, virtually no one is ashamed of what we *are*.

Of course, our sins are very bad. Sometimes they are so bad that we are distracted by them—distracted away from the heart which produces these sins. The Bible teaches that individual sins include such things as malice, envy, lust, drunkenness, theft, hatred, and so forth. These are actions which are performed out in the world. But before any such actions are committed, a human heart must choose them. So the real problem is not the fruit borne by the tree; the problem is the kind of tree that bears such fruit. The things we do are our *sins*. But our *sin* is what we are. We do what we do (commit sins) because we are what we are (sinners by nature). When we come to the point of repentance, we must turn away from both. We must repent both of what we *are* and what we *do*.

Jesus taught us that the nature of the tree determines the kind of fruit it will bear. Because the tree is Adamic, the fruit will always be rotten. We want to pretend that if we only perfume and whitewash the rotting fruit we can somehow change the nature of the tree. Or sometimes people think they can turn over a new leaf by knocking the really rotten fruit off the tree. But the central problem is not the fruit; the problem is the tree. The fruit we bear *reveals* what kind of tree we are, but it does not *determine* what kind of tree we are. An orange tree cannot resolve to be better by growing apples.

So we must pay close attention to what the Lord Jesus taught about this. All Adamic fruit is hopelessly rotten because of the tree it grows on. This means that human nature is *not* basically good.

> Even so, every good tree bears good fruit, but a bad tree bears bad fruit. A good tree cannot bear bad fruit, nor can a bad tree bear good fruit. Every tree that does not bear good fruit is cut down and thrown into the fire. Therefore by their fruits you will know them. (Matt. 7:17-20)

It is an article of faith in the modern world that mankind is fundamentally good and that evil deeds are tragic precisely because they conflict with this inner goodness. But nothing could be more opposed to the biblical view of man. When men sin it is because they are expressing the nature of their inner being. The problem with this inner being reaches all the way back to Adam. The problem is as old as our race and will never be solved through kidding ourselves. We do bad because we *are* bad.

This means that non-believers, as Paul teaches, are without God and without hope in the world. Speaking to the Ephesians, he said "that at that time you were without Christ, being aliens from the commonwealth of Israel and strangers from the covenants of promise, having *no hope* and *without God* in the world. But now in Christ Jesus you who once were far off have been brought near by the blood of Christ" (Eph. 2:12-13). This verse does point ahead to the hope that is offered in Christ, but before we discuss the nature of this hope, we must probe the wound a little more deeply. For the present it is simply necessary to say that our death is in Adam, and the only life offered to us is in Christ.

POINTS TO REMEMBER

• When Adam sinned against God, the entire human race was implicated in that rebellion.

• Adam became a covenant breaker, and in him, so did we.

• We commit sins because we are sinners in our very nature.

• The only way out of this condition is through the work of another Adam.

The Anger of God

We cannot leave our discussion of this problem prematurely. Bad news is always unpleasant, but sometimes it has to be faced in order to be able to appreciate the good news. A certain type of good news can stand by itself—say, for example, you just found out that you won a million dollars in some contest or other. But there is another type of good news which requires a thorough understanding of bad news first. If the governor signed a pardon staying your execution, this would only be good news if you had already understood the news that you were in fact going to be executed.

In the same way, the Christian good news, the Christian gospel, requires a *good* understanding of the *bad* news. And so that is why we have to talk about sin a little more before we turn to the subject of the salvation purchased by the Lord Jesus. Coming right to the point, the Bible teaches us about the holiness and wrath of God. We are not just separated from God; God is angry with us for that separation. We are not just unfortunate; we are rebellious and under wrath.

When we are saved, we are certainly saved *by* God. But what are we saved *from*? The answers to this vary. Some say loneliness, some say the devil, and some say, closer to the truth, that they have been saved from their sins. But the complete answer given in the Bible is that we are saved by God *from God*. The mercy and grace of God saves us from the wrath and judgment of God. Notice how the Bible talks about God's anger: "Behold, the day of the LORD comes, cruel, with both wrath and fierce anger, to lay the land desolate; and He will destroy its sinners from it" (Is. 13:9). The one who will judge is God. The one who destroys sinners is *God*.

This is not because God has a problem with His temper; it is because He is holy. The fact of God's holiness is important for us to establish in our minds before we even consider God's wrath and anger. Without understanding His holiness, we will interpret His wrath as caprice or loss of temper. But on the day of judgment, God will not fly off the handle. His wrath is measured and precise, and it is required by His holiness.

The Bible repeatedly shows us that God is *holy* (1 Pet. 1:15). This word *holiness* refers to all of God's perfections blended together into one attribute, just as the color white consists of all the colors together. But because God is holy, His wrath is holy and is therefore unlike ours (James 1:19-20). This is why the Bible, sometimes in the same breath, talks about God's anger as a good thing and man's anger as a bad thing.

> Because of these things *the wrath of God is coming* upon the sons of disobedience, in which you yourselves once walked when you lived in them. But now you yourselves are to p*ut off all these: anger, wrath,* malice, blasphemy, filthy language out of your mouth. (Col. 3:6-8)

So God's wrath, like God, is entirely holy. The context of this verse indicates that our wicked deeds provoke God's holy anger. However, we must remember what we learned in the earlier section, that our wicked deeds proceed from wicked natures, like foul rivulets from an overfull cesspool. So it is not surprising that our wicked *natures* make us the targets of God's righteous indignation.

We are *all* born under judgment. This includes both Christians and non-Christians. Paul says that we all were "by nature children of wrath, just as the others" (Eph. 2:3). That which distinguishes Christians from non-Christians is *not* the nature we all started with. The believer's only distinction is that he is the subject of the kindness and grace of God. Those who come to faith are removed *by grace* from the lump of clay destined for wrath. "Does not the potter have power over the clay, from the same lump to make one vessel for honor and another for dishonor?"(Rom. 9:21). But by nature, Christians and non-Christians originally come from the same lump of Adamic clay.

Some foolishly entertain comparisons between the Most High God and the chief caregiver down at Buttercup Daycare. But God's ways are higher than ours; because He is holy, He never utters vain or empty threats. Thus, if a non-believer stays where he is, he is separated from God, and consequently he has to face the reality of the wrath of God. If we take a moment to think about these threats in the Bible, they *should* unsettle us—". . . and said to the mountains and rocks, 'Fall on us and hide us from the face of Him who sits on the throne and from the wrath of the Lamb! For the great day of His wrath has come, and who is able to stand?'" (Rev. 6:16-17; Rev. 14:19; 19:15-16).

God's wrath is going to be revealed, and in the day of judgment will fall on everyone who is found outside of Christ. This means that all such persons will *not* inherit salvation.

> For this you know, that no fornicator, unclean person, nor covetous man, who is an idolater, has any inheritance in the kingdom of Christ and God. Let no one deceive you with empty words, for because of these things *the wrath of God comes* upon the sons of disobedience. Therefore do not be partakers with them. (Eph. 5:5-7)

The cross-hairs of divine wrath are fixed on all the sons of Adam, and there is no rock or crevice within which to hide. Nowhere, that is, except in Christ. We are instructed to take refuge from God *in* God. He is our salvation, that is true, but we must realize that He is also the one *from* whom we must be saved.

If we are convinced of this, we take refuge in Christ. Jesus delivers us from the wrath of God. Christians are told to "wait for His Son from heaven, whom He raised from the dead, *even Jesus who delivers us from the wrath to come*" (1 Thess. 1:10). And those Christians who have been justified by the blood of Christ shall "be saved *from wrath* through Him" (Rom. 5:9).

There are only two alternatives: life or death. Life comes through belief in the Son of God, and wrath is the only other option. "He who believes in the Son has ever-lasting life; and he who does not believe the Son shall not see life, but the wrath of God abides on him" (John 3:36).

POINTS TO REMEMBER
• The wrath of God rests upon every descendant of Adam.
• Because of this wrath, everyone who wants to be saved from it must seek a refuge.
• The only refuge from God is found in God.

Who Jesus Is

Now we have said (a number of times already) that our salvation from God can only be found in Jesus Christ, but what does this *mean* exactly? Why Jesus, and why only Jesus? In order to answer the question biblically, we have to address two aspects of the issue. First, we have to consider the *person* of the Lord Jesus Christ, and secondly, we have to consider His *work*.

When we talk about the person of Jesus Christ, we are talking about who He is. What we say about this matters, as it will affect our views of what He did when He died on the cross. We have seen that Jesus Christ is our only refuge from the wrath of God. Outside of Him, there is no hope for us. But if we are seeking refuge from the wrath of God, we need to have more than just the *name* Christ. The Bible says, repeatedly, that we must come to the real Christ, and that there are more than a few fakes. "Who is a liar but he who denies that Jesus is the Christ? He is antichrist who denies the Father and the Son" (1 Jn. 2:22).

Suppose we are talking about a fellow named Bryan, and you say that you think you know who I am talking about. So you describe him; you say he is blond and short, and slightly overweight. I reply, no, he is lanky, has dark hair, and is very tall. We would quickly conclude that we are talking about different Bryans. The name is the same, but the attributes are different. In the same way, many deceivers use the title "Christ," but when they describe his attributes, it becomes quickly apparent that this is a very different Christ from the Jesus Christ of the Bible. Paul had to deal with this problem as early as the first century.

> For if he who comes *preaches another Jesus* whom we have not preached, or if you receive a different spirit which you have not received, or a different gospel which you have not accepted — you may well put up with it! (2 Cor. 11:4)

A different Jesus means a different spirit and a different gospel. This means, boiled down, no gospel at all. The problem with receiving "a different Jesus" is that God has not promised a way of escape from His wrath through anyone who happens to be *called* Jesus. The Jesus Christ who is the refuge from the wrath of God is the Jesus Christ who is described in a certain way in the Bible. Coming to the point, the summary of these biblical descriptions of Him cause faithful Christians to worship Him *as God*. The Jesus Christ who saves is the Incarnation of God. He was fully human, but He was also fully divine.

This means that people who say that Jesus was just a man are talking about someone else entirely. And it does not matter if they say He was a very *wise* man. This is a very important point, and this is why the Bible teaches that this recognition of the deity of Jesus Christ is an essential part of recognizing Him at all. If we do not recognize Him at all, then we cannot be genuine Christians. "*Whoever believes that Jesus is the Christ* is born of God, and everyone who loves

Him who begot also loves him who is begotten of Him"
(1 Jn. 5:1). We see here that a simple invocation of the
two syllables "Je/sus" is insufficient. Jesus is the Christ,
the Son of God, and those who recognize this in truth are
born of God.

So this means we must consider what this title—
Christ—involves. Too many people think of *Christ* simply
as Jesus' last name. But if He had had a last name the
way we do, it simply would have been *Davidson*. In His
humanity, He was descended from King David. But *Christ*
involves far more than this. It is a title, like *King* or *Lord*,
and it means that Jesus Christ is Jesus the Anointed One
of God. As the Christ, He came to reveal who God is and
to accomplish what God wanted done.

> And without controversy great is the mystery of
> godliness: *God was manifested in the flesh*, justified
> in the Spirit, seen by angels, preached among
> the Gentiles, believed on in the world, received
> up in glory. (1 Tim. 3:16)

The salvation of men was a *manifestation*. "And you
know that *He was manifested* to take away our sins, and
in Him there is no sin" (1 Jn 3:5). But this necessitates the
question—manifestation of what? The answer of Scripture
is clear—in Christ, *God* was manifested in the flesh for the
salvation of His people. So this is why it is important for
us to get clear on who Jesus *is* before we discuss the work
of salvation He accomplished. Unless we understand the
appearance of Jesus as the manifestation of God, the great
work of salvation that He accomplished, that of destroy-
ing the works of the devil, makes no biblical sense. "He
who sins is of the devil, for the devil has sinned from the
beginning. *For this purpose the Son of God was manifested,*
that He might destroy the works of the devil" (1 Jn. 3:8).

The manifestation of God in Christ was also a manifestation of love. "In this the love of God was manifested toward us, that God has sent His only begotten Son into the world, that we might live through Him" (1 Jn. 4:9).

Some might want to dismiss such statements as so much irrelevant "theology," but understanding the *Godness* of Jesus Christ is essential to our salvation. Consider the Bible's blunt teaching on this: our salvation rests upon an accurate confession of Christ's identity. *"Whoever confesses that Jesus is the Son of God,* God abides in him, and he in God" (1 Jn. 4:15). A chapter later, the Apostle John puts the same thing another way, "Who is he who overcomes the world, but *he who believes that Jesus is the Son of God?"* (1 Jn. 5:5).

Jesus offers us eternal life precisely because He is the true God in human flesh.

> And we know that the Son of God has come and has given us an understanding, that we may know Him who is true; and we are in Him who is true, in His Son Jesus Christ. *This is the true God and eternal life.* Little children, keep yourselves from idols. Amen. (1 Jn. 5:20-21)

Anything less than this biblical confession is a confession of an idol of some sort (an idol that happens to have the *name* Jesus). And, as the Bible teaches, all such idols are totally impotent and incapable of saving anyone.

So who is Jesus Christ? The Bible's answer is that He is both God and man. All true Christians confess that God became man. The opportunities for clever but wicked men to confuse the issue at this point should be obvious.

> For many deceivers have gone out into the world who do not confess Jesus Christ as coming in the flesh. This is a deceiver and an anti-

christ. Look to yourselves, that we do not lose those things we worked for, but that we may receive a full reward. Whoever transgresses and does not abide in the doctrine of Christ does not have God. He who abides in the doctrine of Christ has both the Father and the Son. (2 Jn. 7-9; 1 Jn. 4:2-3)

I have made this point in various ways many times over for an important reason. Understanding Christ's person correctly, we should see, is essential. It is essential, and yet not sufficient. On the last day, God will judge many rebellious men who had their catechism answers nailed down right smartly. In other words, it is not enough simply to *say* that Jesus is God. We must come to confess this, but simply confessing is not the whole of the matter.

Believing in Jesus Christ as God manifested in the flesh is more than just an exercise in head-nodding. We affirm with our mouths that we believe this, but we are also to affirm with the rest of our lives that we do so. "And this is His commandment: that we should believe on the name of His Son Jesus Christ *and love one another,* as He gave us commandment" (1 Jn. 3:23). Believing in the name of Jesus Christ leads necessarily, the next moment, to a love for other Christians.

This is why the Bible associates "having" the Son of God with having *life*. It involves much more than giving assent to a particular set of propositions. The propositions are important, but they always point beyond themselves. "He who has the Son has life; he who does not have the Son of God does not have life . . . and that you may continue to believe in the name of the Son of God" (1 Jn. 5:13).

In the world of the New Testament, a name was a much greater thing than a mere label. Believing in the name of Christ is inseparable from believing in His true identity.

And believing in His true identity is inseparable from genuine life.

POINTS TO REMEMBER
• Not every "Jesus" is the Jesus Christ of the Bible.
• Jesus is God in human flesh. He is fully God and fully man.
• Those who hold to the truth about Jesus Christ have life.

Christ's Death

In one of his letters, Paul resolved to know nothing except Jesus Christ and Him crucified. He had resolved to preach constantly about the death of Jesus Christ. Some might think that this means that Paul was a simple-minded fanatic. But he does not fit Winston Churchill's definition of a fanatic—one who is unable to change his mind *or* the subject. What it means is that the crucifixion of Jesus Christ is an *enormous* subject. It means that the message of the cross has immense depths which can never be adequately sounded (Rom. 3:21-26). We cannot speak about the death of Jesus adequately without involving everything in the universe, and we cannot truly understand anything in the universe apart from the death of Jesus Christ.

As we consider the death of our Lord Jesus, we must never think of it as something disconnected from God's covenant dealings with mankind. God always works with mankind through covenants. Now by His death, Jesus Christ obeyed God in a way that involves all His people, all the Christians that would ever be Christians, a countless number. The cross of Christ ties these believers together with Christ covenantally.

Now remember, we have already spoken of how Adam represented the whole human race when he *disobeyed* God at the tree. In the same way, Jesus Christ represented a whole new human race when He *obeyed* God at another tree. Adam's disobedience included all his descendants. Jesus Christ's obedience included all *His* descendants too. When Adam rebelled, I rebelled. When Christ submitted, I submitted.

> *I have been crucified with Christ*; it is no longer I who live, but Christ lives in me; and the life which I now live in the flesh I live by faith in the Son of God, who loved me and gave Himself for me. (Gal. 2:20)

Everyone born into the world is a descendant of Adam and shares in his sin. Everyone *born again* in the world is a descendant of Christ, the second Adam, and shares in His righteousness. So being "born again" means that God has brought a person out of spiritual death into life on the basis of the truths we have been discussing.

Remember, because of our connection to Adam, we are all sinners by nature and under the wrath of God. This wrath cannot be avoided. What this means is that the death of Jesus provides a means by which we may die to our condition of death, and rise again. We do not avoid the wrath of God in Christ, we *experience* it in Christ. And so, when we have died with Christ, we are able to rise from the dead in His resurrection, because we share that too.

Outside of Christ, a man is dead and there is no spiritual resurrection. But if we die in Christ, then in Christ we are made alive. The due penalty of our sin is death, and this penalty is not circumvented by Christ; rather, our death is fulfilled in Him. We deserve to die, and by faith, we *do* die—in Christ. But in Christ, there is hope of resurrection. Outside of Christ, there is no escape from the condition of spiritual death. In Adam we die to life.

In Christ we die to death.

In describing the many-faceted character of Christ's sacrifice, Scripture employs a number of different theological words. One of them is "propitiation." The word *propitiation* means that the wrath of God is satisfied. In Adam, God is angry with us. In Christ, that anger is satisfied. And this is how the Bible describes love.

> In this is love, not that we loved God, but that He loved us and sent His Son to be the propitiation for our sins. (1 Jn. 4:10; *cf.* 2:2; Heb. 2:17-18)

In the cross of Jesus Christ, we see the wrath of God poured out upon sin and all sinners who are in Christ. It is crucial for us to realize that there is *no propitiation* outside of Christ. This means that wrath remains on everyone who remains outside of Christ.

Another aspect of Christ's sacrifice which the Bible emphasizes is that He is our "redemption." The word employed here would have brought images of the slave-market—the buying of slaves—to the minds of its original readers. Those who trust in Christ are freed from slavery to sin. The death of Christ is also described in Scripture as a *ransom*—a payment which purchased us. Our redemption is through Christ's blood. "He has delivered us from the power of darkness and conveyed us into the kingdom of the Son of His love, *in whom we have redemption* through His blood, the forgiveness of sins" (Col. 1:13-14).

So for those who are forgiven, this redemption is the ground of their glory. "But of Him you are in Christ Jesus, who became for us wisdom from God—and righteousness and sanctification and redemption—that, as it is written, 'He who glories, let him glory in the LORD'" (1 Cor. 1:30-31). In other words, Jesus became our redemption so that we might glory in Him.

A third concept that the Bible emphasizes when speaking of Christ's death is that of "reconciliation." Reconciliation refers to the establishment of peace where once there was enmity or hostility. The Bible says God was in Christ, reconciling the world to Himself in the death of His Son.

> Now all things are of God, *who has reconciled us to Himself through Jesus Christ*, and has given us the ministry of reconciliation, that is, that God was in Christ reconciling the world to Himself, not imputing their trespasses to them, and has committed to us the word of reconciliation. Now then, we are ambassadors for Christ, as though God were pleading through us: we implore you on Christ's behalf, be reconciled to God. For He made Him who knew no sin to be sin for us, that we might become the righteousness of God in Him. (2 Cor. 5:18-21)

So Christ's death was a propitiation that turned God's wrath away; a ransom that purchased our freedom; an act of reconciliation that brought peace between His people and the Father. But in all this, Jesus Christ had more than good intentions. His sacrifice didn't just make these things a possibility it rendered them *certain*. When Jesus went to His death, He was not attempting anything. He was not giving the salvation of His people "a try." He knew beforehand the power of what He was going to do. He was going to destroy the devil and save the world.

> 'Now is the judgment of this world; now the ruler of this world will be cast out. And I, if I am lifted up from the earth, will draw all peoples to Myself.' This He said, signifying by what death

He would die. (John 12:31-33)

So Jesus was not dying on the cross in order to make salvation a mere *possibility*, but rather actual. This actual salvation was accomplished for all who believe in Him. Consider how the Apostle Paul thought of this.

> Therefore, as through one man's offense judgment came to all men, resulting in condemnation, even so through one Man's righteous act the free gift came to all men, resulting in justification of life. For as by one man's disobedience many were made sinners, so also by one Man's obedience many will be made righteous. (Rom. 5:18-19)

Paul is doing here what we have mentioned numerous times already. Christ is an Adam, and His obedience had the same kind of *effectual impact* on His descendants that Adam's sin had on his.

POINTS TO REMEMBER

• In the cross of Jesus Christ, the wrath of God is satisfied. This is called *propitiation*.
• In the cross of Jesus Christ, His people have been purchased, or *redeemed*.
• In the cross of Jesus Christ, a *reconciliation* between God and man is accomplished.

Christ's Resurrection

The resurrection of Jesus is far more than just a "happy ending" to a tragic story. The resurrection was a part of God's plan from the beginning; it was an essential part of what had to happen. Those who do not see the importance of this are still "slow of heart," as Jesus would say.

The resurrection is crucial to the Christian message of salvation. The early church knew this better than we do today, and so they preached the resurrection of Jesus often. When the first disciples were discussing the replacement of Judas Iscariot, one of the things they were concerned with was the need for an eyewitness to the *resurrection* (Acts 1:21-22). The resurrection of Jesus was one of the great points of Peter's sermon on Pentecost, the first sermon of the Christian era. As he put it, *"This Jesus God has raised up,* of which we are all witnesses" (Acts 2:32).

The Athenian philosophers even thought that Paul was preaching foreign gods (Acts 17:18) because he preached of Jesus and of *Anastasis* (the Greek word for resurrection). They thought there were two gods here—Jesus and Anastasis. When they finally figured out that the point being made was that the resurrection was an element of the Christian gospel, these unbelievers quickly mocked (Acts 17:32). Nothing really changes; they mocked it then, and they mock it now. Paul considered himself persecuted because of his preaching of the resurrection (Acts 23:6-8). In short, the preaching of the resurrection was an integral part of the apostolic message.

We should first note that they preached the resurrection *of* Jesus. "And with great power the apostles gave witness to the resurrection of the Lord Jesus. And great grace was upon them all" (Acts 4:33). But secondly, as a consequence of this, they preached resurrection *in* Jesus. "Now as they spoke to the people, the priests, the captain of the temple, and the Sadducees came upon them, being greatly disturbed that they taught the people *and preached in Jesus the resurrection from the dead"* (Acts 4:1-2).

Thus, we modern Christians also declare that Jesus rose from the dead. Because He rose from the dead, we can preach a general resurrection from the dead, a resurrection of all men. If this message is not true, then after we go into the ground, we simply rot.

Modern men tend to think of the resurrection of Christ as something which needs to be proven. This element certainly is present in the biblical account (i.e., Christ proved Himself to His disciples after the resurrection), but the Bible also presents the resurrection as a powerful proof in its own right.

First, Christ was proven to be the Judge of the earth in His resurrection. This connects the resurrection to our earlier discussion of other elements of the Christian message—our sinfulness and depravity.

> Truly, these times of ignorance God overlooked, but now commands all men everywhere to repent, because He has appointed a day on which He will judge the world in righteousness by the Man whom He has ordained. *He has given assurance of this to all by raising Him from the dead.* (Acts 17:30-31)

In other words, the resurrection is not so much something that needs proving, but something which does some proving. In this case, the resurrection proves that Jesus is the One who will judge the world.

Secondly, God proves who Jesus is through the resurrection. Recall what we said earlier about the identity of Jesus being an essential part of the Christian message. That identity is declared within the gospel by the resurrection of Jesus from the dead.

> . . . concerning His Son Jesus Christ our Lord, who was born of the seed of David according to the flesh, a*nd declared to be the Son of God* with power according to the Spirit of holiness, *by the resurrection from the dead.* (Rom. 1:3-4)

So we see that the resurrection declares Christ to be the Son of God and the coming Judge. But it also has implications for our legal standing before this Judge. In talking about this new legal standing, the Bible uses the word *justification*. Those who have believed in Jesus Christ have a new standing before God in the resurrection of Jesus Christ.

> Now it was not written for his sake alone that it was imputed to him, but also for us. It shall be imputed to us who believe in Him who raised up Jesus our Lord from the dead, who was delivered up because of our offenses, *and was raised because of our justification.* (Rom. 4:23-25)

Put simply, all believers died in Jesus Christ in His death on the cross and rose again with Him in His resurrection. This happened through our covenantal connection with Him. He died, and so we have redemption. He rose, and so we have justification.

In this passage just quoted above, we see the connection between the death of Christ and our offenses. We also must see the connection between His resurrection and our justification. Remember that the word *justification* refers to a new legal status—what is that status? The answer is that of a convicted criminal, tried and executed, and now raised. If a criminal were to be executed for his crime, and then rose from the dead, he could not be tried again. He would have a new legal status.

Just as the resurrection affects our justification, so also it affects our sanctification. Sanctification is the word the Bible uses to describe the process that Christians go through as they become progressively more like Jesus Christ throughout the course of their lives. Put simply, sanctification is the process of growing in *goodness*.

The words *justification* and *sanctification* are distinct, and yet closely related to one another. Just as a husband is different from his wife, yet without a wife he is no husband, so justification is different from sanctification but is not justification without sanctification. In the same way, justification is distinct from becoming good, but if there is no process of growing in goodness, then this means there has been no justification.

> Therefore we were buried with Him through baptism into death, that just as Christ was raised from the dead by the glory of the Father, even so we also should walk in newness of life. (Rom. 6:4)

Christ was raised from the dead in order that believers could *walk* throughout the course of their lives in newness of life. His resurrection was the foundation of their justification, but it was also the basis for their growth in newness of life. Thus we may properly say that the resurrection is also the foundation for the Christian's ongoing life in Christ.

POINTS TO REMEMBER
• The resurrection of Jesus Christ establishes that He will judge the entire world.
• The resurrection of Jesus Christ shows that He is the Son of God.
• The resurrection of Jesus Christ is the basis of a new standing in the eyes of God.

A Right Response

From our vantage, everyone who hears these truths is called to respond to them by repenting of their sins, and believing in the Lord Jesus Christ. This is simple on paper, but the sinful heart makes it tangled and complex.

To maintain our footing, we must remember the ground of our salvation. Just as we are lost through our union with Adam, so those who are saved are saved through their union with Christ in His perfect life, death, burial, resurrection, and ascension. When we speak of the ground of salvation, we are talking about the *basis* for it, the *foundation* of it. Everyone who comes to salvation is saved because of the person and work of the Lord Jesus Christ, plus nothing else. His work, and God's grace in uniting us with Him, is the sole reason we are saved.

Salvation is in and through Jesus Christ alone. But does this mean that we do *nothing*? If we are to do something, is that something "our part" which is the partner with God who then does "His part"? Not at all. Of course, we are called to do something (repent and believe), but everything we do is built upon the foundation of Christ's work. We are not to extend our work from Christ's work; rather, we are to build our work *upon* Christ's work. We do not build out, we build up.

But wait, some are thinking, we *do* contribute to our salvation. Faith is our contribution, isn't it? On the contrary, faith—the instrument of our salvation—is itself a gift of God. This distinction between the ground of our salvation and the instrument of our salvation is only possible if faith is *God's* instrument for saving us, not our instrument for getting the job done. If it were our instrument, then our wielding of that instrument would necessarily become part of the ground of our salvation—that upon which our salvation rests. But like axle grease and ice cream, grace and works do not mix.

> Even so then, at this present time there is a remnant according to the election of grace. And if by

grace, then it is no longer of works; otherwise
grace is no longer grace. But if it is of works, it
is no longer grace; otherwise work is no longer
work. (Rom. 11:5-6)

The Bible's testimony about this is not opaque. Apart
from repentance we cannot believe, and apart from faith
we cannot be saved. Both repentance and faith are gifts
from God. First, we see that if someone has true repentance, the Bible speaks of that repentance being granted to
them. "When they heard these things they became silent;
and they glorified God, saying, 'Then *God has also granted
to the Gentiles repentance to life*'" (Acts 11:28). The Apostle
Paul speaks the same way.

And a servant of the Lord must not quarrel but
be gentle to all, able to teach, patient, in humility
correcting those who are in opposition, if *God
perhaps will grant them repentance,* so that they
may know the truth, and that they may come
to their senses and escape the snare of the devil,
having been taken captive by him to do his will.
(2 Tim. 2:24-26)

The same thing is true of faith. If someone has faith in
Jesus Christ, it is because God gave it as a gift. "For to you
it has been *granted* on behalf of Christ, *not only to believe in
Him,* but also to suffer for His sake . . ." (Phil.1:29). Luke
describes Christians as those who have believed *through*
grace, not believed *in* grace.

And when he desired to cross to Achaia, the
brethren wrote, exhorting the disciples to
receive him; and when he arrived, he greatly
helped *those who had believed through grace;* for
he vigorously refuted the Jews publicly, showing from the Scriptures that Jesus is the Christ.

(Acts 18:27)

Of course, there is a very famous verse on salvation which makes this same point—"For by grace you have been saved through *faith,* and *that* not of yourselves; *it is the gift of God,* not of works, lest anyone should boast. For we are His workmanship, created in Christ Jesus for good works, which God prepared beforehand that we should walk in them" (Eph. 2:8-10).

The very first good work that believers were created for is conversion—turning away from sin in repentance and turning to God in faith. This work we do because we are God's workmanship, and the work we do was prepared beforehand by God so that we could walk in that work. What is the work of God? "Jesus answered and said to them, 'This is the work of God, *that you believe* in Him whom He sent'" (John 6:29). The good news here for any reader is that if your heart is turning away from your sin and toward God, this is an indication that God is *already* showing His kindness to you.

Points to Remember
• Repentance is a change of mind, rejecting both sin and all sins.
• Faith is trust in God's provision of salvation in the death and resurrection of Jesus Christ.
• Both repentance and faith are necessary for salvation.
• Both repentance and faith are gifts from God.
• Whenever a sinner asks for these gifts, the answer has already been granted.

The Sum of the Matter

I trust that the teaching of the Bible on the salvation of sinners has been made plain. I also hope that any non-Christians who have come to read this have worked carefully through this booklet with pen in hand, marking any questions they might have and making notes where necessary. But more is necessary than simply laying out the facts. Even if they are true facts, even if they point to the kindness of God, the kindness of God remains to be tasted and experienced. When all is said and done, an invitation to believe is necessary, and the tone of the invitation will have to be different than a careful rehearsal of the facts. "Now then we are ambassadors for Christ, *as though God did beseech you by us*: we pray you in Christ's stead, be ye reconciled to God" (2 Cor. 5:20). I *plead* with you to turn to Christ, and I must alter my tone to do so.

The Lord Jesus Christ was called Immanuel by the prophet Isaiah, and that name means *God with us*. These three words together contain depths which no mortal mind can really fathom. Proud reason never enjoys the sensation of coming to the end of its tether. *God* with us? But God has revealed this truth to mankind, and we are required to meditate on it. Good food for sinful men lies here, but we must take it as it has been prepared. The good Lord has invited sinful mankind to dine, but never to cook. But when we eat what He has prepared, it is a joyful feast.

At the birth of Christ, the angel gave the shepherds "good tidings of great joy . . ." (Luke 2:10). Great joy has always been a hallmark of real Christianity. Peter affirms this: "Though now you do not see Him, yet believing, you rejoice with joy inexpressible and full of glory . . ." (1 Pet. 1:8). Frankly, the joy many nominal Christians feel is joy expressible, not joy inexpressible, and certainly could not be described as full of glory. But you are not being invited by Christ to nominal Christianity, that is, a bland salvation, or a tepid justification. At the heart of the Christian message is joy—joy to the world, joy that is fierce, joy that can't change the subject.

This message of great joy is for all people (Luke 2:10). This is not truth for a select few. The gospel message is not the password into a tiny mystical band of true believers. Jesus did not come into the world to be the founder of some backwater mystery cult. We must understand that the entire world is the intended recipient of God's redemptive blessing. The message is for the world; Jesus came for the *world*, and consequently, there is joy to the world. He did not come for the Jews alone. He came and suffered and died for all men. But still less did He come to bring the possibility of joy; He came to bring joy. He did not come with potential salvation for the world; He came with salvation for the world. He came to accomplish this salvation, and He has done so.

In this planet of darkness, a great river of light has sprung forth. That light has now come by you and is flowing right next to your feet. The blessing will continue to flow on, a great, growing inexorable river, until it engulfs all peoples, tribes, and nations in the joy of Christ. And if God is merciful to you, it will engulf you as well.

The river has a fountainhead. The reason for our joy is found in the identity of the Christ as Lord and the mission of the Christ as Savior (Luke 2:11). The angel said that He was a Savior, but whom does He save? And from what? The answer to these questions is found when the angel of the Lord appeared to Joseph and told him to give the name Jesus to the unborn child. "And she shall bring forth a Son, and you shall call His name Jesus, for He will save

His people from their sins" (Matt. 1:21). So whom shall He save? He will save His people. And from what shall He save them? He will save them from their *sins.*

But what is sin? The Bible gives us a complete and sufficient answer. "Whoever commits sin also commits lawlessness, and sin is lawlessness" (1 Jn. 3:4). It is a hard definition, at least when we see it without the devil's varnish. God, our Creator, has the absolute authority to dictate to us the terms and conditions of our lives. Sin is nothing more or less than the refusal to recognize and submit to that authority in any area.

Through His death, Christ saves His people from lawlessness. They are saved, first, from the lawlessness itself. When Christ saves a man, that twisted man dies, and a new man replaces him — "if anyone is in Christ, he is a new creation; old things have passed away; behold all things have become new" (2 Cor. 5:17). He is saved, secondly, from the penalty connected to his previous lawlessness. That penalty was death. Adam was told that the day he ate of the fruit of the tree in the middle of the garden, he would surely die. Ezekiel tells us that the soul that sins shall die. Paul states, unambiguously, that the wages of sin is death. But in saving His people, God does not waive the penalty of death. Christ died as the covenant head of His church and paid the penalty for their sins in full.

But is this all *true*? Before answering the question, we must alter it. We must not ask what is true. If we want the biblical answer, we must ask *who* is the truth. In Scripture, truth is not an abstraction. Truth is real; truth lives, and truth has a Name. Autonomous men in all ages have always sought to ignore this. Pilate cynically asked, "What is truth?" when the living embodiment of Truth was standing right in front of him. How often this happens! Blind men stare at the truth in front of them, say they see no truth, and then go on to crucify it.

The Eternal Word of God, the Eternal Truth, in obedience to His Father, took on human flesh. We Christians call this the Incarnation. There was a day when Truth came into the world; Truth has a birthday. "The Word became flesh and dwelt among us . . ." (John 1:14). In the first verse of that chapter, John says the Word was God. And then he says here the Word took on flesh. We must think about this. What did John mean by *Word*, and what did he mean by *flesh*?

This divine Word truly took on flesh; it was no apparition. Consider the reality of what Christ's first followers saw. They heard Him; He spoke to them. They saw Him; His body reflected light. They touched Him; He was no ghost. And what was it they heard, and saw, and touched? It was that which was from the beginning; it was the Word of life. And this Word of life, this Eternal Truth, was visible, in just the same way that a table, tree, or you are. So this baby, this child, this man, was God enfleshed. The infinite put on finitude, and lost nothing. The immortal one put on mortality, and purchased a people for Himself. The invisible God shows Himself to us in His visible image, Jesus Christ, the exact representation of His being.

If Jesus was only a man, He was not the apostle of God. If He was only God, He was not the High Priest we needed. Thus it is that the God/Man is our Savior; only He is strong to save. And we should remember the last sentence of 1 John 1:4, "And these things we write to you that your joy may be full." There is that result again—*joy*.

What must we think about this? What must we do? There will always be those who want to avoid such great questions. But like a blind man who falls in the ditch, it doesn't much matter what side of the road the ditch is on. If you stay on the road, it may be instructive to listen to these ditch-bound guides as they debate the relative merits and advantages of each ditch.

One group says that we should be more practical. Why all this preaching about doctrinal and theological stuff? Why can't we just have a simple inspirational message? The answer of the Bible to this objection is plain — *that* kind of simple "inspirational" message is false. That kind of simple message is for those who have itching ears. "Peace, peace," is a simple message, but the prophet Jeremiah tells us there is no peace. Some men in the New Testament said that a man had to be circumcised to be saved. That is simple enough for God to damn it. *Repent and believe in the Lord Jesus Christ* is also simple, but in an entirely different way.

Our race fell in Adam. The reality of this problem confronts us everywhere. A glance at a newspaper is more than enough to confirm man's sinfulness. But the original source of the problem, Adam, and our relationship to him, is not at all simple to comprehend. Why were we born with a bent toward sin, just because of what *he* did?

The infinite Word of God took on human flesh and walked around in our midst. This is complicated doctrine which the wisdom of this world calls foolishness. But what does God command us to see? There, look at Infinitude in a manger born to be Infinitude on the cross. There is only one sense in which this message is simple. It is simple to declare, and because it is the power of God to salvation, it is simple to believe. But in no way is it simple to understand. Those who demand a message simple to understand are still worshipping their idols.

But let us not forget the group in the other ditch. They want to avoid practical obedience. They are willing to talk theology and doctrine. They are willing to study it for years. They are willing to take degrees in it and establish institutions to grant degrees in it. But are they willing to live what they profess? It's certainly worth talking about!

True doctrine properly received brings joy. Such doctrine imitated brings humility. But how can we receive and imitate a doctrine? Because doctrine is truth, and the Truth is the Lord Jesus Christ, we must receive *Him* as the One who reveals the Father. We are to receive Him, our only hope of salvation.

The Point of Decision

These truths about sin are a message of consternation and dismay. How can they be the foundation of a great and eternal joy? There was born that day in the city of David a Savior. For those still in sin and blindness, there is hope born in Bethlehem. For those who still cling to carnal reasoning, there is an infinite Savior, there, in the feeding trough. But this Savior is not an abstract proposition; He is a Person, and you must come to *Him*. So come, in your mind, to Bethlehem. Like the wise men you bring something, but unlike them, the gifts you bear are not at all precious. Instead of gold, you bring the filth of your own corruptions. Instead of frankincense, you bring a life of pride and self-centeredness. Instead of myrrh, you bring your desperation and sorrow. You come as a supplicant and not as a donor.

Now, look on that baby, unable to speak—the Eternal Word, unable to speak. Now look to Mary. She was told, at the very start, that her heart would be pierced through with many sorrows. You know, after the fact, what those sorrows involved. Through God's foreordained and perfect plan, a horrible crucifixion was accomplished by wicked men. You think of that death, which was a death for sinners, and you look down at your own filthy, grimy hands. Think again about the infant Christ; the child is mortal. There is breath in his nostrils; there is movement in His limbs. This child, because He is a child, is capable of *dying*. And then it becomes clear—He was born to die. He was prepared to do His Father's will, which happened to be submitting to His own murder, predestined before the origin of time. In that murder we see the salvation of the world.

For those who understand the Word of God, something has happened. If your heart has been touched by the Spirit of God, you will call upon the Lord. You will understand, for the first time, that the great joy promised to the shepherds is a particular kind of joy. It is the joy that comes from forgiveness and cannot exist without a prior misery and desperation.

Now look around that feeding trough. It may have been a stable or a courtyard—we don't really know. But whatever it was, it wasn't much: a newborn infant, lying in a feedbox, in an obscure jerkwater town, two thousand years ago. But because it wasn't much, it is an appropriate place for a sinner to kneel down and pray.

But in order to pray, a man must have a warrant to pray. He must have received an invitation.

An Invitation

We have all received invitations, and we have all responded to them—one way or another. When one is invited somewhere, he either goes or he doesn't. Once an invitation is given, a response of *some* sort is required. Not to respond is in itself a response.

Sometimes, when a host wants to know how we regard his invitation, he will ask for the courtesy of our response beforehand. He will usually indicate this through the letters R. S. V. P. somewhere on the invitation. When someone receives an invitation like this, they do not make the decision whether to attend the banquet the night of the banquet. The banquet is planned, the invitations are sent, and the responses are gathered *beforehand*.

This is what the kingdom of heaven is like. The King has planned a great feast. He has sent out His messengers, and they are authorized by Him to issue a general invitation. This booklet was written by one of those messengers, and it is appropriate to conclude with some of the marvelous invitations of Scripture.

One of the most striking invitations is found in the prophet Isaiah:

> Ho! Everyone who thirsts, come to the waters; and you who have no money, come, buy and eat. Yes, come, buy wine and milk without money and without price. Why do you spend money for what is not bread, and your wages for what does not satisfy? Listen diligently to Me, and eat what is good, and let your soul delight itself in abundance. Incline your ear, and come to Me. Hear and your soul shall live; and I will make an everlasting covenant with you—the sure mercies of David.   (Is. 55:1-2)

Isaiah offers here an invitation, and he contrasts it with the foolishness of refusal. Here are the terms of his invitation: If you are thirsty, you may drink. If you are poor, you may nevertheless buy and eat. You may buy wine, and you may buy milk; the lack of money is no problem at all. Isaiah knows that those who are considering this invitation have no money and no food. They have no money and no drink.

So what does a refusal involve? Instead of bread and

wine by grace, the foolish man scrapes out his pennies, and then purchases *panis sordidus*, bread full of sawdust and wine full of water. What little money he has goes to buy food that is no food; *it does not satisfy*. The prophet is baffled; why do you *do* such things? The wine is here, the bread is here, and the bill has been paid. *Come and eat! Come and drink!*

In the book of Proverbs, in the ninth chapter, we find a set of invitations. One comes from Wisdom, the woman who lives in a house of seven pillars. She cries out: "Whoever is simple, let him turn in here!" To the one who lacks understanding, she says, "Come, eat of my bread and drink of the wine which I have mixed. Forsake foolishness and live, and go in the way of understanding."

This is in contrast with the invitation given in that same chapter by a foolish woman. *She* says, "Stolen water is sweet, and bread eaten in secret is pleasant." Folly loves to speak in this way. Bread and water taken in rebellion are sweet. The great Lady, Wisdom, is *giving* away wine, and the foolish man spends all that he has to get some putrid water. The bread of life is offered to all, but some don't want the gift. They only want what they can steal. They only want that to which they have no right.

The Lord Jesus gives a wonderful invitation in Matthew 11:28-30. It is the same kind of invitation as those we have been considering. He says, "*Come to Me*, all you who labor and are heavy laden, and I will give you rest. Take my yoke upon you and learn from Me, for I am gentle and lowly in heart, and you will find rest for your souls. For My yoke is easy and My burden is light."

In the previous verse, our Lord says that no one knows the Father except for those to whom the Son wills to reveal Him. Now some have vainly, and foolishly, sought to discover who these people are by prying into the secret counsels of God Most High. But for those who are content not to blaspheme, the identity of these people is revealed in verses 28-30. The Great Invitation is God's ordained means of identifying, in the eyes of the world, those who belong to Him, that is, those who will enjoy His feast on the great day.

So who belong to Him? Those who *come* because they labor and are heavy laden. These are people under the burden of sin and self-centeredness, and they want out from under the burden. Who belongs to Him? Those who *come* and take *His* yoke upon them, and agree to learn from Him. Who belong to Him? Those who *come* and find rest for their souls under a yoke that is easy and a burden that is light. This is in sharp contrast to the yoke they are carrying before they come to Him. These are His—the ones who come.

Now hear this plainly. *You* are invited. There is one thing you must remember from this message, this invitation. It is this: *You are invited.* But this information, like all knowledge, can be abused and twisted. It is important to remember the nature of the invitation—it is not open-ended. You had no claim on the invitation to begin with, and now that you have received it, you must remember your duty with regard to it.

He has invited all men, and therefore *you* must respond. Simply receiving the invitation is not adequate. Look there on the bottom. You can see it plainly enough— R. S. V. P. There are many who will go off to the outer darkness clutching their by-then worthless invitation. In their blind folly, they preferred to eat the paper than the bread of life.

What about you? I trust this foolishness will not be yours. Will you come? *You have been invited.*

But some of you may be wondering at the nature of

this invitation. You see no piece of paper with your name on it. How can you know that you have been invited? Is this nothing more than the invention of some preaching writer?

If you are of this mind, there are three things you should consider:

First, you can know that you have been invited if you understand that you meet the conditions set by Scripture. Wisdom invites you to turn from folly; have you been foolish? The prophet points out that sinners labor for bread that is not bread; is this not you? Are you not tired of bread that does not satisfy? And by now you should be really sick of that colored water that your friends think passes for wine.

The Lord Jesus invites those who are weary from labor; is this not your condition? He beckons to those who are heavy-laden; do you not qualify?

There should be no disputing it. *You are weary.* You are weary of your husband, or of your wife. You have been faithful to them, and you are tired of that faithfulness. Or you have been faithless, and you are tired of that. You are weary in your employment. When you get up to go to work, it has more than once occurred to you that you don't know why you do it. But more than just your work is affected; you are weary in your amusements and diversions.

You look at your children, and you are weary of them. You feel guilty, but guilt cannot take away weariness. The guilt is simply one more weariness. Only One can take the weariness away.

When you think about your life and what a pitiful waste it is, the wisdom of *another* preacher, from an ancient time, is driven into your heart. All is futility; everything is vanity and striving after wind. *Everything* they told you was a lie. They said you could have it all, and it is beginning to look as though you will end your life with two fistfuls of wind and a large bill for the coffin.

What did the great king Solomon have? He had wealth, he had women, he had godless feasting and high culture. All of it, he concluded, was a waste. What does he say about it? "For what has man for all his labor, and for the striving of his heart with which he has toiled under the sun? For all his days are sorrowful, and his work grievous; even in the night his heart *takes no rest.* This also is vanity."

Think and consider. What profit is there in gaining the world and losing your soul? If you gain the world, you have nothing but a great ball of futility and confusion. As you consider these things, you realize your weariness. Our Lord Jesus describes your condition; you know that His description is accurate. He says that you labor, and you know that you do. He says that you are heavy-laden, and you know that you are. He knows that you are in desperate need of rest for your soul. Why do you not agree? *Therefore,* the description fits; the invitation has your name on it.

In the second place: you can know you have been invited because this booklet is in your possession through obedience to the command of God—the invitation has come to you. In the gospel of Mark, Jesus tells his followers to *go and preach.* He says, "Go into all the world and preach the gospel *to every creature.*"

His command is plain enough. You are created by Him; you are therefore a creature. You are in the world; you have lived here your entire life. This was written by a messenger of Jesus Christ, who has presented the gospel to *you,* in obedience to His command. The authority to issue such an invitation has been granted, and it is consequently not rude or impertinent for you to respond. Indeed, it is rude and impertinent *not* to respond.

On another occasion, our Lord told a story about a great feast and how those who were invited first declined to come. So then the master of the feast commanded his servants to scatter all over and invite *just anybody*. So here, you have been found out, the Word has sought you out; you are invited to come.

You cannot avoid the invitation under this heading. The messengers of Christ carry His Book, and they preach His gospel. Are they preaching from this Book? Do they tell you of a crucified Savior? Then their credentials are good, and *you* are invited.

You may feel there must be some mistake; the messenger has come to the wrong person. Not at all. You feel yourself to be insignificant? That presents no problem at all. The messengers have been especially instructed to seek you out. What does the Apostle Paul say?

> For you see your calling, brethren, that not many wise according to the flesh, not many mighty, not many noble, are called. But God has chosen the foolish things of the world to put to shame the wise, and God has chosen the weak things of the world to put to shame the things which are mighty; and the base things of the world and the things which are despised God has chosen, and the things which are not, to bring to nothing the things that are, that no flesh should glory in His presence. (1 Cor. 1:26-29)

So, then, this invitation is in your hand because you have read these words. There is no escape from them. You must begin to consider how you are going to respond.

And lastly, you can know the invitation is for you if you believe that this is the truth. Those who receive the invitation do not have to wait until they *die* in order to know they have eternal life. They can know *now*, in this life. Not only can you know in this life, you can know that you are invited in just a few moments. The Apostle John says that he wrote down his words so that believers could *know* that they had eternal life.

The Apostle Paul tells the man who had imprisoned him in Philippi that if he would believe on the Lord Jesus Christ, *he would be saved*. Throughout the New Testament, we find this message again and again, over and over. *Repent and believe*. Associated with this requirement, we find the promise—no one who believes in Him will be put to shame. All who call on the name of the Lord will be saved.

Here is another way to think of it: God has given His promise to save sinners. He will save *any* who repent and believe. If you do this, then His promise applies to you. If you refuse to believe it, then what do you care? It is a matter of indifference to you whether it applies or not. But those with stony hearts do not ask such questions.

So here is the Word of God for tender hearts. There is no way for someone to believe the promise, only to find out later that there was some confusion on the matter and that they were not really invited. So long as God is true, such a thing cannot happen.

So do you believe that this message is a true word from God? Then the invitation is for you. You will not be turned away at the door. You will not be embarrassed. *You are invited*.

Perhaps you think these invitations are the ravings of madmen and fanatics? Then whether the invitation is yours is no concern of yours—and will remain such until you repent and believe. But if you believe this, then there is certainty; the invitation is for you.

Wait for a moment. The invitation is for you, and you

have been told that you have a duty and obligation to respond. You have also been told how you can be confident in responding to this invitation. But you have not yet been told *how* to respond.

When you receive invitations from men, they have on them an address or phone number. There is no real difficulty in knowing how to respond. This, however, is a spiritual matter. The invitation is a spiritual one. You have read some *writing* about God's invitation and how it is an invitation which includes you. But you have thought it over, and have realized that you do not have God's address. Suppose you wanted to respond to His invitation. How is this thing done?

In the gospel of John, chapter 12, Jesus says this about His upcoming death, "And I, if I am lifted up from the earth, will draw all peoples to Myself." The apostle goes on to declare that Jesus was signifying what sort of death He would undergo. That death was a crucifixion. Jesus was hanged on a cross and lifted up from the earth.

But it is interesting to see that Jesus prophecies that this death on a cross of wood will have an effect on all peoples; they will, as a consequence, be drawn to Him. This is how you respond to the invitation: you come, you are drawn, to the cross of Jesus Christ in faith.

It is also interesting to note that you can see here, in your own heart, a fulfillment of this prophecy. Are you not drawn to Him? Did He not say that this would happen all over the world? Here you are, two thousand years later, and the death of a Jewish carpenter still has an immense power. If it has power to draw *all* men, and it does, will it not have the power to draw *you*? Look to your heart—you can see it happening.

So here is the message; Christ died for sins according to the Scripture, He was buried, and He was raised to life on the third day. And this is the invitation; you are invited to believe what I have just told you. The man who believes in his heart that God has raised Jesus from the dead *has responded to the invitation.* The man who confesses that Christ was hanged on the cross, under the weight of sin, *has responded to the invitation.*

It is impossible to respond to God's invitation without believing that Christ was a substitute for sinners on the cross. The man who seeks to come to the banquet without faith in a sin-bearing Christ will be thrown into the outer darkness —he is not appropriately dressed. He has not been washed in clean water and is not fit to eat the bread and drink the wine. He must be washed through the forgiveness of sins, purchased for him by Christ in the redemption of the cross, and he must be dressed in the righteousness of Christ, which was won for him in the resurrection. If he is not, then he will be robed in nothing but despair, and pitched headlong into the darkness. So how is he to be dressed in such righteous apparel? How is he to put such things on? He is to *believe* the message; he is robed in Christ *by faith.*

So what will you do with these things? You have heard of a crucified Savior, a Savior who was lifted up. What do you say? There are only two possible responses: *yes* or *no.*

You still say no? And why? You say that the way is hard. You do not wish to begin, only to fall away from Him. But salvation is from the Lord. The One who saves is the same who keeps. If you call on the name of the Lord, you will be saved. Not for a short time, and not temporarily. *Saved.* You will have eternal life, as a present possession, bestowed in eternity for all eternity.

You say that you are defiled? That you are not worthy to come? But there never was a sinner who *was* worthy! Defilement must not keep you from coming; defilement is the *reason* you must come. Come, and be clean! Come, and be washed! Come, and welcome!

You say that God does not want you? that you are not predestined to come? But the Lord says that whoever comes will not be cast out. What prevents you? Those who do not come refuse merely because they love their sins more than God. Is this true of you? Then stay away, and welcome to it. If your confused and stupid heart wants nothing more than to gnaw on bones and blackened crusts when the table is set, and the bread of life awaits, then go ahead and refuse the invitation. But do you want to be free of your lusts and desires, your weariness of heart, your malice and bitterness? Then *come.*

You say that you do not yet believe? Ah, but you do. There are no unbelievers; there are simply those who believe and hate, and those who believe and love. Which are you? You have read about a Savior, hung on a tree, drawing all men to Himself. What do you make of Him? You *do* believe, but a question does still remain. Do you *love* this Savior or not? Yes or no?

You say you are uncertain as to whether He loves you? The question is an impertinent one and proceeds, just like the rest of your sinful life, straight from a black heart—as though any sinner *ever* deserved His love! The question that must be answered today is not whether He loves *you*, but whether you love Him. If you love Him, you will keep His commands and do His work. And what is His work? It is that you believe in Him, and only Him. And when you have come to this love, through faith, you will realize that you only love Him because He *first* loved you.

You say that some of your sins are too great to be forgiven? Your pride, at least, is great. *What?* You think that you, a mere creature, are capable of sinning in a way that would bankrupt the grace of God? He offers you this grace; do you want to accuse Him of being a cheat? Do you think you could come and find God's storehouse empty? Proud man, your sin is great enough to damn you, but it cannot be greater than the grace of God.

You say that a loving God would not send you to judgment? But is God love, and nothing else? Is He not also just? And how can a just God allow someone like you into His presence? The judgment is simple; there are no problems caused by it. Sinners deserve to be cut off, and they are. *But grace!* There is the problem. How can a God of justice tolerate proud men? The answer to this problem is the cross. God sent His Son to die on the cross, so that He could be just *and* the One who justifies. So we come to this place again. Do you believe or not? Do you do the work of God at this place or not? If you turn away, then God remains just, and *you are undone*. But if you call upon Him, the One who died, God remains the One who justifies, and you will be the one justified. What do you say to this? Yes or no?

You say that you need time to think. Maybe you will come later. Maybe this is not the right time. Remember as you turn away from Him, that your heart is deceitfully wicked. It is *lying* to you. Your heart sees you looking at the cross there, and it sees you thinking about it. But for your lying heart, the cross is the way of death and only death. *Tomorrow*, it whispers. *Not now.* Do not be hasty; do not run into anything too quickly.

What does Scripture say? Does God know what your heart is saying to you? Aye, God knows. And what does He say? He says that *today* is the day of salvation. No one ever got saved tomorrow, and not one soul was ever pulled from the edge of the pit yesterday. *Today* you hear, and *today* you must believe. Which is it: yes or no?

You say that your friends will mock, and that your

family may not come with you. That is true; they may not. They may *all* turn from you, and reject you. But again, what does Scripture say? If you love father or mother, wife or children more than the One who died for sinners, then you cannot come. God does not want you on *your* terms. He commands you to count the cost; thus far you are doing well. But He also commands all men everywhere to repent. Why do you hesitate at this? Why do you halt? *He commands it.* And what do you think of His commands? You are a creature, after all. Which is it, yes or no?

You say that the church is full of hypocrites? I say that everywhere you turn you see the cross, and so you turn away from it again. So how, proud sinner, do you differ from the hypocrite? He knows what is true, but does not do it. *You do the same.* Christ is the Savior of the world. You know it, but you do not repent. You know it, but you do not believe. You hypocrite! Will you posture and make a show of how much you hate hypocrisy? It is only a covering for *your* hypocrisy. Or do you only hate hypocrisy when it belongs to another? So we cannot leave the point alone. The Savior is there; He has died, no, more than that, He has risen to life. But what do you say? Yes or no?

You say you want a preacher who will make you feel good about yourself? Ah, but is there any good reason why you *should*? Should sinners be told they are not sinners? Should sinners be left in their blindness? But the truth is unpleasant, you say. *So it is.* But it remains the truth, and what do you say? Yes or no?

You say that people should not come to Christ out of fear of hell. On the contrary, this is an excellent reason to come, and the One who sent out all His messengers agrees. Did He not say we were to fear the One who can throw both body and soul into hell? Do you not fear Him? Consider the logic of your unbelief—"I do not think people should take medicine merely because they are sick and are going to *die*. I do not think a man should appeal to a judge for mercy simply because he has been *condemned*. I do not think . . ." But that is enough folly. What do you say: yes or no?

You say that there are people who have never heard about this Christ? You wonder if God is just in His condemnation of them? He is just, for these people you speak of do not love the truth any more than you do. But God is full of mercy and has commanded Christians to preach to them, as well as to you. After you have believed, perhaps *you* will be sent to them. It is clear you have a great compassion for them; you still hate God yourself and are yet concerned for *them*. So what will it be, yes or no?

You say there are many religions. You wonder why this religion is pressed upon you. Because you need saving and this is the only one which has the power to save sinners. And why does it have the power to save? Because it is God's truth and is nothing to be ashamed of. It is the power of God unto salvation, for everyone who believes, and in that "everyone" is an invitation for you.

We could continue this for a long time, but you should be impatient with your own excuses. But that is no matter, we are only men. What does it matter if we tire of these excuses? But there is a day coming, and it is coming for everyone who hears Christ's voice, when *God* will have had His fill of your excuses. What is that Day? It is the day you leave your life here and walk into His Presence, naked, alone, sinful, and ashamed. What will you say? You will have no Advocate. Will you successfully present the excuses of your heart here today? Or will those excuses be consumed in the Judgment *along with you*?

If you say no and set this booklet aside, then are you saying that you are willing for this to happen? I suppose that is good, *for it will happen*. You will have no ground for complaint when it does.

But if you say yes, then what is the gift? You, out in the cold of your malice, out in the dark of your lusts, have been shown a great house. The Master of the house has invited, no, more than that, *commanded* that you come and fellowship with Him at His table. But there, out in the night of your sin, you have hated Him. For years, you hated His wealth, you hated His charity, and you hated His sons and daughters. But now, by the Spirit, beyond your understanding and mine, that hatred is gone. You approach the door, trembling and afraid. It is a huge door, but no, it is not locked; it swings open. Bright, warm, yellow light streams out. The heads at the table turn in welcome, and you wonder *why* you hated them. No servant has to scurry to set a place for you; *the place is already set*. The Master beckons for you to take your seat. You try to protest; your clothes are filthy, and you have not been washed. But then you look down and see that you are dressed in clothes you have not seen before, and they are *white*. Your hands are *clean*.

You turn around and look back out the door. You remember now, with a burning shame, all your excuses. You remember now all the times the Master of the house invited you to come—but you would not. You remember the mystery of your own sinfulness and wonder why you did not come before. You turn back to the table and take your place, your eyes full of grateful tears.

You look at the food and wonder at the simple fare. There in the middle is the bread of life. The one who eats will never be hungry. There in the goblet is a deep, red wine. The one who drinks will never thirst again. You shake your head in wonder at your own blindness and at the mercy of God in removing it from you. *Truth is bread,* and it feeds the hungry. *Truth is wine,* and it takes away the dry parched thirst in mouths of sinners. You, dear friend, bow your head to say grace, and you will say it forever and ever, world without end. Amen.

As another preacher said, centuries ago, come, *and welcome,* to Jesus Christ.